A. HOPE

Embracing the Unknown

Reflections and Insights from a Marriage Challenged by Mental Illness

Contents

1

To the Reader

Thank you for picking up this book. I hope the reflections and insights from my experience with mental illness and its impact on my marriage are of some worth. Due to the nature of mental illnesses, this book will mention or discuss in varying degrees of detail symptoms related to the specific diagnoses of my spouse, including suicidal ideation. This is not easy to write, nor is it easy to read. And since you are reading this you either have or are currently going through something similar - your spouse or loved one has been diagnosed with a mental illness. If so, I am sorry you are going through this.

First, I want you to know that it is OK.

- OK to be afraid, because this is scary.
- OK to be anxious, because tomorrow, the next hour, the next minute is so uncertain.
- OK to be angry, because this has interrupted your plans for a season or more.
- OK to cry, because this hurts.

Mental illness is cruel to patients and significant others alike.

Second, if your loved one or any of you in the household are in physical danger, get help immediately.

Next, you can seek help and guidance from trusted family, friends, church/community resources, and professionals.

Finally, as you will see in the following pages, you can't manage your loved one's mental illness. You can, however, manage your response to it. And this is where you have power and control.

Take care of yourself. It's time to embrace the unknown.

A. Hope

2

Stepping on the Path

In the Beginning, I Was Clueless

"I wish you could just be happy."

We were driving home from an enjoyable dinner and church activity. At least, for me it was. My spouse, however, was looking rather down and had been for some time.

Of course, my charming, logical self proceeded to explain all the reasons my spouse should be happy:

- We have a roof over our heads.
- We have food on the table.
- We have three beautiful children.
- We have good health.

Or, so I thought.

I grew up believing we had control over our thoughts, words, and actions.

I never realized there are people who, at times, cannot control their behavior.

I found out firsthand, over the course of several months, how true that is, how confusing that is, how scary that is - and how ill-prepared I was for what transpired.

At my insistence, my spouse tried to be happy, but no matter what was done nothing worked.

My spouse tried to exercise. Nope.

My spouse tried healthy eating. Nope.

My spouse tried being with friends. Nope.

My spouse wasn't unhappy. My spouse was depressed.

Depression is difficult for the whole family. It changes the dynamics of your relationships. It changes the day-to-day functions of running a household.

My spouse could no longer contribute to our partnership of marriage.

And I became frustrated.

Then, my spouse began to change.

My spouse had energy again. Cleaning was getting done. Working on more projects. Spending more time with family and friends. There was more laughter. More talk of spiritual matters.

Life was feeling pretty good.

But it wasn't happiness, it was mania.

Speech became rapid and pressured. Shopping became more impulsive. Sex became concerning, not exciting. Sleep was gone. The nights were filled with deep cleaning or getting closer to God. Every interaction with someone was in the context of saving their soul.

What happened next terrified me.

My spouse experienced suicidal ideation, attempted to claw into the wall to hide from the world, and began to explode at me in fits of rage that lasted hours.

We went to the emergency room. And I experienced what no couple should, but many do.

I went out one exit and my spouse went out another to be escorted by ambulance to the psych ward.

I sat in our car and cried.

Our lives were changed forever.

This Is Scary. Where Is My Support?

"After weeks of in-patient and out-patient care we have determined your spouse has Bipolar Disorder Type 1, Post-Traumatic Stress Disorder, Dissociative Identity Disorder, and severe anxiety. Do you have any questions?"

I reached forward to grab the small packet of papers from the counselor's stretched out hand.

The room wasn't tiny, but it was simple.

My spouse and I sat on a small couch. The counselor sat across from us in a large living room chair. These rooms are designed with the intent to make the discussion more comfortable, like sitting at home. But that doesn't really work.

"Tell us about the medicine."

I honestly didn't have any questions. I didn't know where to start. How could I? This "thing" came out of the blue, was scary, confusing, and damaging. And I had no idea how to process any of it.

"Well," the counselor began looking at my spouse, "you will take medicine for the rest of your life."

"So, there is no cure?" I asked with a look of emptiness, I'm sure. I was so tired.

"No. You will live with bipolar for the rest of your life. You will have to learn to manage it. What other questions can I help you with?"

What I experienced that day, but did not realize at the time, is that our mental health system in the United States is not designed, nor equipped, to support the spouses of those diagnosed with a mental illness.

Our meeting with the counselor was brief. The follow-up was none. The resources provided were geared towards the patient. And zero consideration for me, our marriage, or our children.

I felt so alone. It shouldn't be that way. But I had to do something.

I Can Fix This, Right?

Because I was totally beside myself.

As shock gave way to space for questions to flood my mind, beginning with, "What the hell happened?!" I began to develop a resolve that this was never going to happen again. I went into fix it mode.

I began changing everything in life. I moved the bedrooms around. I integrated new technology into our apartment to improve lighting and natural ambient noise. I adjusted my work schedule and location. I took on all of the household responsibilities and care of the kids. I did it all!

I told myself that if I changed our lives, I can prevent this from happening again.

I was wrong. And it took me almost four years to finally accept that I cannot fix this.

So I Can Handle This, Right?

All too often we convince ourselves and others that we are ok. We say things like:

- "I've got this."
- "We're doing fine."
- "It's just a little tough right now."
- "I'll get through this."

We do this because we don't necessarily want others to know. We are afraid if others know what's really going on we'll lose them (which may happen). We don't want the "label" on our relationship. We don't want this to become our identity.

However, becoming the caretaker can become consuming, and pretty soon "this" becomes your identity.

You forget who you were. You forget what you enjoyed doing. You lose contact with loved ones. You begin to wonder, "Where am I? What happened to me? I don't even know who I am anymore."

When mental illness takes up residence in your marriage, you lose yourself trying to handle all of it on your own.

My spouse was hospitalized in October of 2018, and our lives were turned upside down.

Our marriage of ten years received new partners: Bipolar Disorder Type 1, Post-Traumatic Stress Disorder, Dissociative Identity Disorder and severe anxiety.

And life was never the same again.

I thought I could handle it all on my own.

I worked to financially support the family. I was responsible for all of the cleaning, cooking, and care of the children. I got the family to our church activities. I kept up a facade. In reality, I was falling apart.

My feelings toward my spouse became resentful. My faith in God dwindled. My children became lightning rods for emotions I did not know how to process and release. In short, I no longer recognized myself. Two years in I had to take action; so, I took these three steps:

- I began therapy.
- I began writing in a journal.
- I began connecting with others who had been there.

I learned I was not alone. I learned I could adjust. I learned I could heal.

I learned I could connect with my spouse in new ways.

And I learned these three steps were important to take when my life was first turned upside down, not two years in.

Lessons learned, and others that follow I hope will help you on your journey.

Committing to Your Partner, You Commit to Their Past

When you commit to a partner, you also commit to their past, their coping mechanisms, and their [communication] style. Choose wisely. They will [have] the greatest impact on your overall mental wellness.

This tweet from @Theholisticpsyc sums up my naiveté.

For years I expected my spouse to change behaviors.

I needed my spouse to stop.

Stop blaming me for things I didn't do. Stop treating me like a garbage disposal for everything that is wrong in life. Stop putting me on the shelf when you're done with me. Stop taking me off the shelf when it's convenient. For the love of God, stop complaining!!!

Because I have feelings, too - and this is exhausting.

What I didn't know was that an unknown past lurked within.

My spouse shared that someone once asked them to disrobe - and they shouldn't have.

This person should have been safe. This person should have been trustworthy. This person should have been a protector.

Instead, this person created a past. 10 years into our marriage that past finally introduced itself.

The cycles were long in the beginning. For weeks or months my spouse lacked energy to do anything.

Cleaning was a burden. Caring for the kids was a burden. Intimacy was a burden. My work was a burden.

Then bursts of energy appeared seemingly from nowhere that lasted a few days, maybe a week.

Cleaning our apartment at night. Taking the kids on adventures. More expressive during intimacy. More supportive of my endeavors.

And then anger, particularly towards me. And I honestly didn't know why. Within a day or two, however, that anger shifted to the person that should have been trustworthy.

This cycle repeated, with the duration shortening with each instance. Then came hospitalization and diagnosis. And a new journey began.

At first I still put this journey solely on the shoulders of my spouse.

They had to communicate better. They had to take their meds. They had to attend their therapy. They had to manage their sleep. They had to own their journey.

All of this is true. But I learned I had to change, too.

I had to communicate better. I had to manage my expectations. I had to reimagine what marriage is to me. I had to set boundaries and keep them. I had to own my journey.

But because we both committed, today we have a healthy relationship and marriage.

So, how is this possible?

I Learned 3 Hard Truths

Before 2018, I was unaware of the possibility of mental illness at our age (late thirties). It wasn't on my radar. I was focused on finances, career, and family - with three kids under the age of seven. I was thrown a curve ball when my wife shared her first suicidal ideation with me.

After a few weeks of in-patient care, we received the following diagnoses: Bipolar Disorder Type 1, Dissociative Identity Disorder, Post-Traumatic Stress Disorder, and severe anxiety.

Now that the mental illnesses were named I began researching. I Googled. I read books. I listened to podcasts. I asked questions.

But as my research expanded my inner peace with the situation did not.

The more information I consumed the more I began to question what was really going on. I became more confused, scared, and angry with the curveball life threw me. And I wasn't sure who or what to believe.

That is when I learned 3 hard truths about how confusing mental illness is.

Hard Truth #1: There are no medical tests to confirm mental illness diagnoses.

There are tests to confirm diseases like cancer, diabetes, influenza, and COVID; but none for mental illnesses.

Mental illness diagnoses come from evaluation and long-term observation from a dedicated treatment team. The psychiatrist monitors and adjusts medicine. The therapist leads sessions. The medical doctor tracks other physical conditions. The spouse (or significant other, as we are called) shares observations with the treatment team.

This is a journey of trial and error and patience - and it takes years.

Hard Truth #2: Mental illnesses share symptoms.

If you Google "I have a stomach ache what could it be" the results list conditions that share the same symptom.

Mental illnesses, too, share symptoms. Agitation, irritability, anger, sadness, trembling, panic attacks, outbursts, and other uncontrollable behaviors. These can all be common with anxiety, depression, mood disorders, personality disorders, trauma disorders, etc. So, which one is it?!

This is when I learned the next hard truth.

Hard Truth #3: My response to the symptom was more important than which mental illness caused it.

I made a lot of mistakes responding to the symptoms of my spouse's four mental illness diagnoses.

I did not know what was going on. I was confused, scared, and angry. I was defensive, insensitive to, and invalidating what my spouse was feeling and expressing. I am learning to set boundaries; communicate clearly and regularly; support, but not fix; validate, but not agree with; take care of myself; and ask for help when I need it.

This multi-year journey is making me a new person.

By learning these 3 hard truths, I am now experiencing more peace in my journey as we work together to manage mental illness in our marriage.

3

Symptoms Are Often Scary

Symptoms Are Confusing and Appear Out of Nowhere

Have you seen those charts which list the current symptoms for COVID, influenza, and RSV? They are almost identical! So, which does the patient have?

I feel the same way with symptoms of mental illnesses, which manifest similarly.

I was on the receiving end of narcissistic behavior during my spouse's manic episodes. I began to question if there was a misdiagnosis, because the behaviors were identical. What I acknowledged is that when a person vomits the disease could be anything. The same is true with symptoms of mental illness - which is it really?

The following are three experiences with some of the symptoms of bipolar many may relate to.

Rapid Speech and Suicidal Ideation

"You spoke for 45 minutes straight really, really fast. I couldn't get a word in. And I don't think you took a breath."

Driving home from work that day was different from previous commutes. Something was off with my spouse. Speaking 45 minutes straight wasn't uncommon, but this was rapid speech. And the amount of topics covered? Honestly, I don't remember.

What I do remember is saying to myself, "What is happening?!"

I decided it was time for a date.

I asked my spouse to get ready to go out to dinner, just the two of us. It took me another 20 minutes or so to arrive home. The apprehension was building, but I was still more curious than anxious at this point. I observed other odd behaviors in the weeks leading up to our date, and I began mapping them out in my mind.

Rapid speech was a new piece to the puzzle I was trying to assemble, only I didn't have a picture to reference.

The rapid speech continued during dinner, only the topics were more concerning.

I learned that my spouse wasn't feeling well. Happiness was gone from life. My spouse's only desire and goal was to go home to Jesus. The method considered earlier in the day: driving into an on-coming train. Suicidal ideation was another piece to the puzzle.

I should have taken more concrete action right then, but I didn't - and I regret that.

A day or two later we were in the emergency room.

My spouse spoke with such speed that the nurses couldn't get a word in. During one "discussion" my spouse suddenly stopped. I looked at the nurse and said, "Did you see that?" referring to the rapid speech. A simple "Yup" was the response.

Sleep was the prescribed remedy; it never came.

We returned to the emergency room, then my spouse was admitted to the psych ward.

Hyper Sexuality: The Bipolar Symptom That Challenged Me the Most

"I need you to leave the room. I have to tell the nurse something erotic."

I stepped out of the emergency department triage room and took a walk down the hall.

You might think that questions would begin flooding my brain.

Who is my spouse sleeping with? Is it unprotected sex? How long has it been going on?

But they didn't.

Looking back, I think I was in shock.

I felt confused. I felt scared. I felt sad.

I was in a state of disbelief.

I turned around and saw the nurse.

I walked back towards the room. The nurse invited me in, but didn't say anything. I took a seat next to the bed. My spouse appeared in a daze. I remained in the dark.

We sat in silence, listening to the rhythm of the monitors.

The preceding event happened a couple more times while in the emergency department.

My spouse asked me to leave so I wouldn't hear the erotic thoughts shared with the nurse. I walked the hall. I returned and sat in silence.

But now I started thinking.

Sex has been different lately.

My spouse initiated - a lot. Stamina was high. Different positions were tried. Other rooms and furniture were "broken in". Self pleasure was engaged in.

After ten years of marriage and three kids, sex became a novelty in our relationship.

The sex should have been exciting, but it wasn't.

We were engaged in amazing sex. We were trying new things. My spouse was initiating!

What more could I want?

Sex was happening in the midst of other concerns.

My spouse was impulse buying. My spouse wasn't sleeping at night. My spouse had bursts of anger and rage. My spouse's mission was to bring everyone to God. My spouse was experiencing suicidal ideation.

What my spouse was doing during sex was out of the norm in our relationship.

I later learned what the erotic thoughts were.

My spouse was so wound up with sexual tension that the only desire was to be admitted to the psych ward and have sex with everybody.

And I was introduced to hyper sexuality - the bipolar symptom that challenged me the most.

Spiritual Grandiosity: How Mania and 9 Letters Introduced Me to the Devil

"Do you see these letters?"

"Yes," I replied.

I had sat down on the love seat only moments before. Exhaustion had taken hold of me; I needed rest.

The living room was in disarray.

Kids' toys were strewn across the floor. Unfinished art projects and crafts lay on the coffee and end tables. Laundry overflowing baskets. (Which basket is clean and which is dirty?) Dishes with leftover food from the morning's breakfast remained untouched, laying where there was space and no space.

A reflection of our lives.

Mania consumed my spouse a few weeks before; the second episode that year. It began with little temper tantrums. Each argument, however, became more intense and abusive as the agitation increased and sleep decreased.

The current medicine regimen was not working.

"What do the letters mean?" I asked as I leaned forward to read the notebook. Incoherent statements and chicken scratch covered the pages. But near the bottom of the right page were 9 letters surrounded by white space.

The letters read: "TDWUMTDY"

"This is an acronym," my spouse said as the index finger moved across the letters.

"It means, 'The devil will use me to destroy you.'"

Well, this is going to get interesting. We had experienced grandiosity and hyper-religiosity before, but this was different.

Rather than my spouse getting closer to god, the devil was here to destroy me.

In the coming weeks, this played out in a real way. The mania, paranoia, and delusions had become hyper-focused on me. I was the enemy.

Then it happened. My mind broke, and I began weekly personal therapy. And my spouse began anti psychotic medication.

Episodes Vary in Duration and Intensity

2020 was a very long year.

Yes, the world battled the COVID global pandemic. That is what 2020 will be remembered for. But for me, my spouse's manic episodes define that year.

See the illustration in the thread that gives you a snapshot of 2020 for me.

Manic episode 1 duration: ~ 6-8 weeks

The first episode included a hospital stay.

I'm not quite sure when this episode started. It felt like a slow onset that climaxed with sex (no pun intended). Our intimacy triggered a dissociative experience in my spouse. Congratulations, Creating Quietude, you're now one of them.

I am a creator of alters.

But the other alters had something to say.

The next morning, the alter that was raped in my spouse's early 20's was fronting. By the time we made it to the hospital, the 3-4 year old sexually abused alter was fronting. Communication was reduced to incoherent mumbling and blowing raspberries as the medical team scrambled.

Three days later, on Valentine's Day, my spouse was released and we went to dinner.

Manic episode 2 duration: ~ 12-14 weeks

Then summer arrived.

Beginning about mid-June, my spouse's maturity level dropped to that of a hormonal teenager - rebellious, argumentative, and rude.

Hyper sexuality made intimacy problematic, not enjoyable.

The mood swings were exhausting.

Delusions and paranoia abound.

Hospitalization was narrowly avoided with the addition of an anti-psychotic medicine.

That day, my spouse's first abuser passed away; the episode lasted another 4-6 weeks.

Manic episode 3 duration: ~ 16-18 weeks

The reprieve was short lived; maybe a couple of months.

The holidays are stressful already; they can also be triggering. Then throw in a move. This episode also felt like a slow roller. It didn't peak until February/March the next year.

We closed out the year manic.

Mental illness is cruel. For those managing bipolar, mania, in particular, leaves many deep wounds.

4

Coping When Symptoms Are Bad

6 Ways I Cope With My Spouse's Mental Illness

Walking this path has been so difficult. Coping has been a struggle for me. Honestly, I don't want to cope. What I really want is for this to go away.

I want the trauma to go away. I want the abusive behavior to go away. I want the feelings of loneliness and isolation to go away. Nevertheless, coping is a must. Here is what I have applied in my life.

Coping Mechanism #1: I go for walks.

I walk for at least thirty minutes every day outside. I feel my best, however, when I walk for ninety minutes each day. This isn't all at once; it's usually from two-three walking sessions each day. And at my pace, this is well over the recommended 10,000 steps we should take each day, which is the equivalent of six miles.

Coping Mechanism #2: I write in my journal.

Sometimes, especially during a manic episode, I perform a brain dump multiple times a day. There is so much happening that I had to write down as a record of what transpired. The chaos of these episodes will cause events to blur. It is important to write them down. Other times, however, I doodle or sketch in my journal.

As I've reviewed my journals over the years I noticed that I became very diligent in documenting all the negative that was happening. However, they are very scant on any positive experiences during that time.

I invite you to also write down the good moments, even if you have to look harder for them during certain seasons.

Coping Mechanism #3: I attend therapy.

I highly encourage you to have a therapist. Mental illness wreaks havoc on marriages, and there is a lot to unpack. It would be beneficial to find a therapist that is experienced in both marriage/family counseling and the diagnoses you are navigating.

Coping Mechanism #4: I vent.

I don't do this often. I feel like I am complaining when I do. Perhaps I do need to vent more often though. Find a trusted friend or family member you can vent to. Consider venting to your therapist. I also found some online therapies provide an environment to vent in.

Bottom line: Give yourself permission to be angry and let off some steam. Vent!

Coping Mechanism #5: I cry.

It is OK to cry, right? I don't do this very often, either. But my safest place to cry is in the shower. I have found I always feel better after I cry for a while.

Coping Mechanism #6: I share experiences with other people.

In addition to talking to my therapist, family and trusted friends, I join communities with others who have gone through or are currently going through what I am. This helps remind me that I am not the only human on planet earth who is going through this. I know I am not alone.

5

Owning My Part of the Journey

I Waited Too Long

My biggest mistake was waiting to get help for myself and my mental health.

Here are 3 things I wish I did on day 1:

Begin therapy.

I waited about two years before I began seeing a therapist. By then I had developed

- Anxiety
- Depression
- Trembles

Don't wait to process what is happening. Begin therapy immediately.

Find informative resources.

For me, I read <u>When Someone You Love Is Bipolar</u>, by Cynthia G. Last, Ph.D. It was about two years before I found this book, and it made all the difference. I gained insight into:

- Bipolar symptoms
- Coping strategies
- Managing expectations

Grab this book today! Research other books that are pertinent to your situation. Keep in mind that some mental illnesses and disorders do not have as much written on them, yet. It may be difficult to find a quality book. But as many of these mental illnesses share symptoms and their impacts on relationships are similar, this book may be of value to you, as well, even if your spouse or loved one is not diagnosed with bipolar disorder.

Join a community.

I waited about three years before I joined a community. I felt so alone before I did. There are some amazing online communities on Reddit I recommend you research, based on your specific situation.

Once I joined a community I now knew I:

- Wasn't alone,
- Was validated in my experience, and
- Was able to support others.

These made all the difference. I wish I started sooner.

Together, but Single - A Paradigm Shift

When one can't, the other must.

However, you become overwhelmed.

You take care of your spouse. You take care of the cooking. You take care of the cleaning. You take care of the laundry. You take care of the kids. You take care of the bills. You take care of making money.

You become the caretaker.

Six months after my spouse was hospitalized with mania, I was at a total loss.

At that time we had three kids under the age of 7. My spouse could not contribute in a meaningful way. My job was over an hour away, with a total average commute of 3 hours per day. I came home to nothing done around the house. Everyone was hungry. No one was bathed.

Resentment towards my spouse was building rapidly.

Then one day I received an impression: "Live your life as a single, full-time working parent."

"Come again," I said.

"Live your life as a single, full-time working parent."

That doesn't make any sense. I am married. My spouse should be a contributing partner in this marriage; physically capable of all that needs to be done.

I was so naive, and I resisted the impression.

Another six months goes by, and my resentment builds.

On the flight home from what I have labeled as the worst vacation of my life the impression came again: "Live your life as a single, full-time working parent." I decided right then and there I would do as the impression said. I began researching online for what single parenthood actually means. I paid more attention to single parents that I knew. I sought counsel from family, friends, and mentors.

I began the journey to change my mindset and reimagine my situation.

The result was nothing but a miracle.

It didn't come all at once, but as the weeks went on the resentment lessened. Compassion towards my spouse grew. I was a happier, more present parent and spouse.

I found my burden lightened.

I am grateful I (finally) gave heed to the impression. It changed me, and it changed my marriage during that season.

The Unconventional Advice I Received That Set Me Free

"In sickness and in health." Said by millions, this simple phrase in the traditional wedding vow inspires. You picture future milestones of a healthy life together.

The stay-in date nights, filled with intimacy. The vacations you take together. The birth of your children. The purchase of your home. The celebration of a big promotion at work. The kids are leaving home to begin their lives allowing the two of you to redefine your lives as empty nesters. The fifty year wedding anniversary, and growing old together.

This is the "in health" portion of the vow.

We create fewer pictures for "in sickness," however.

Standing next to your spouse, your hand on their back, as they get sick into the toilet. A late night in the emergency room, receiving care for an unexpected injury. And, maybe, sitting next to a hospital bed, holding your spouse's hand as they are treated for one of the big ones, such as cancer, heart disease, and diabetes.

We avoid contemplating the "in sickness" portion. That is scary, and who wants to think about those unpleasant topics? And for many, mental illness and its impact are not even considered.

At this point in my journey, it had been almost two years since my spouse was diagnosed - and I was exhausted. Two hospitalizations. Numerous hours of therapy. Adjustments to medication to find the right regimen. But still the struggle was real; it was bad; and there was no end in sight.

But I kept reminding myself, "In sickness and in health. I have vowed to be here for my spouse in sickness. And the scriptures say these pains are only temporary." However, that "sickness" was destroying me.

I was the garbage disposal for my spouse's pain and rage. I was constantly emotionally and verbally abused. I was accused of doing horrible things. I was lied to, cursed at, and manipulated. Nevertheless, I kept my vow of "in sickness and in health" - as I understood it. Then I gained a new perspective.

I met with a trusted friend and spiritual advisor. He had been walking this journey with each of us, and was very aware of our situation. I expressed my doubts of our marriage enduring this trying time. That I feared being a failure. That I was going to break my vow if I divorced.

He then said something, although unconventional to me, I will never forget: "You can still keep your vow, it just may not be with your current spouse."

At that moment I felt a tiny portion of my burden lifted, as if he had removed a stone from the large pack of rocks on my back. I began to reimagine my wedding vow for my situation.

Yes, mental illness falls into the "in sickness" portion of the vow. Yet, mental illnesses, particularly those involving mood and personality disorders, can be immensely destructive to relationships, because of abusive behaviors. And I was abused. (Wow, that's hard to say!)

And abuse is not inherent in the marriage vow.

Now, it was as if I had given myself permission. I no longer felt trapped by a vow that my spouse wasn't reciprocating. I didn't have to endure abusive behavior anymore. The power was within me to change. I didn't feel like a failure if I moved on.

And it set me free. This is when I really started to focus on healing me and reimagining my marriage relationship.

6

Strengthen Your Relationship

Show Them You Care, Even if They Mistreat You

"Just tell me you are going to stay with me. Even if you have to lie, tell me that you are not going to leave me."

I am taken aback. I don't know how to respond. But I had to say something.

"Well, I am still here."

We looked into each other's eyes.

It was different than before. We used to look longingly with passion and joy at one another. We saw hope in a future we were building together. Laughter, playfulness and intimacy accompanied such moments. But now it was uncomfortable.

Almost two years had passed since Bipolar Disorder and Dissociative Identity Disorder moved into our marriage.

The past several weeks had taken their toll.

Mania raged. Paranoia controlled. Chaos reigned.

And my spouse feared abandonment more than anything else.

I made a lot of mistakes.

I internalized my spouse's words. I avoided one-on-one time to escape. I never set boundaries to safeguard my mental health.

Needless to say, this was a disaster.

But I learned a few lessons to show someone with mental health issues that you care.

First, I learned that validating feelings does not mean you agree with the words spoken.

When someone is managing a mental health issue they struggle to convey properly what they actually mean to say. In the case of my spouse fear of abandonment, caused by childhood trauma and sexual abuse, was the feeling at the root of all the hurtful words said. I took these as personal attacks, rather than sitting in the pain my spouse was trying to heal from.

A better response would have been, "That must be really scary to feel like the person you love is going to leave you."

This validates that being abandoned is scary. It does not, however, mean that the feeling was based on facts.

Validating feelings shows someone with mental health issues that you care for them.

Next, I learned that setting aside one-on-one time brings confidence to the relationship.

Mental health issues can lead someone to feel lonely, unwanted, and unworthy. These messages can lead to a "self-fulfilling prophecy" as they begin to push loved ones away. To escape the burden I would spend more time with the kids or exercising, rather than giving my spouse undivided, loving attention.

A better option would have been to schedule one to two hours, once or twice a week, specifically to grow emotional intimacy.

This emotional intimacy, sans sexual intimacy, helps develop a confidence and trust in the relationship.

Setting aside one-on-one time shows someone with mental health issues that you care for them.

Finally, I learned that setting boundaries is caring for both of you.

Someone managing mental health issues may find themselves hurting their loved ones with unfiltered speech. Not only do the words cut deep, but they fly at you like a locust devouring a field of grain. And for my part I just sat and took it.

A better option would have been to set a boundary, which might look like this:

"I am hurt when you call me names. When that happens I am going to pause our conversation. I will take a 30 minute walk around the neighborhood. When I return we will continue our conversation."

Setting boundaries shows someone with mental health issues that you care, because you also are caring for yourself.

Mental health issues impact so many relationships.

You can show someone you care by validating feelings, setting aside one-on-one time, and setting boundaries.

By doing so, you will strengthen your relationship one feeling at a time.

3 Levels of Discussion: A Simple Framework for Successful Communication

The single most important factor to a successful relationship is communication.

Through early communication we decide with whom to build a relationship with, and filter out others. That communication broadens and deepens strengthening the relationship. Eventually, communication becomes the key to achieving life's goals in an intimate way within the relationship.

Without communication, our greatest adventures are not supported, experienced, nor shared with the ones we love.

However, Bipolar Disorder complicates and clouds communication.

The dark rain clouds of depression dampen the dreams once shared in the relationship. The exuberance and intensity of mania and its potentially destructive symptoms challenge the stability of the relationship. And the sometimes irrational and hurtful comments create fear and distrust.

The relationship, therefore, becomes confusing and hopeless.

The key to improving communication is to simplify.

Life continues so coordination is required. As consuming as Bipolar can become, for much of the time we still need to touch base with our loved one on a daily basis. We also have to spend time diving a little deeper and working on emotional intimacy in the relationship.

Simplifying communication to focus on these three areas helps the relationship maintain a foundation when times get tough.

Level 1: Logistical / Coordination.

Life continues, and you get to function in it with as much normalcy as you can.

Except for the most difficult and scariest of times managing Bipolar, your lives continue as normal with the flare Bipolar brings to the mix. It is still important to coordinate work, appointments, and kids' activities. Hold this at least once a week for just the upcoming week, with regular syncs as the week progresses.

This logistical coordination discussion provides a sense of "normalcy" in your relationship.

Level 2: Daily Touch Base.

Your relationship still exists, and you need to show each other you care.

Focus on only two or three questions that express your interest in your partner's day. These questions may include:

- How was your day?
- How are you feeling today?
- Would you like to share with me what you did today?

Put parameters on this discussion, too. For example, you each only get 10 minutes to discuss your day. Staying within the framework removes pressure from engaging in an unbridled brain dump.

This daily touch base discussion provides a sense of "care" in your relationship.

Level 3: Deep Dive.

Sitting together in deeper conversations can strengthen intimacy.

Identify one or two nights a week to sit together and talk for one hour. Put it on the calendar in your coordination discussion. During the discussion, remove distractions such as technology or other interests. If you have kids, see if a family member or friend can watch them. Take this time to explore each other's feelings and experiences over the past week. Approach the discussion through the lenses of compassion and curiosity. You may learn something new about your partner and yourself.

This deep dive discussion provides a sense of "intimacy" in your relationship.

The Importance of Boundaries.

Even with this simple framework, the realities of Bipolar are ever present.

Mood swings are real. Each of these discussions is susceptible to them. This means unfiltered and emotionally draining conversations can ensue. Protect yourself by setting a boundary.

For example, if name-calling takes place you could say, "I am hurt when you call me a jack wagon. I need some space. I am going on a walk around the neighborhood. I'll be back in 30 minutes. We can continue the conversation when I return."

Just because you are in a conversation, trying to follow this framework, does not mean you have to listen to emotional and verbal abuse. Take care of yourself.

With all that said, consistent effort leads to improvement.

Everyone can communicate. But to communicate well takes practice, especially in a Bipolar relationship.

You will make mistakes. It is impossible not to. You have to give yourself grace and try again.

Keep at it and you will develop a simple framework for successful communication with your Bipolar significant other.

Setting Boundaries in Your Relationship

Let's face it, mental illness creates an environment of "walking on eggshells." And you want nothing more than to take a break. For me, a break is creating distance between myself and my spouse over an extended period of time with minimal to no contact. In some instances, this might exactly be what is needed. However, often what we need is just a little space - a short period to clear your thoughts so you can re-engage with your spouse.

What might that look like for you? Here are some steps to take:

First, identify your boundaries. At what point does an argument become too much for you? Is it the tone of voice, the volume, the use of name calling or vulgar and demeaning remarks, incoherence, or the length of the argument? Your boundary may be, "I'm not OK with raised voices during conflict."

Second, define what "space" means to you. Ask yourself three questions:

- What will I be doing?
- Where will I be doing it?
- How long do I need?

My "space" is taking a 30-minute walk around the neighborhood alone.

Third, practice what to say. You are going to have to explain this to your spouse at some point. It may go something like this:

"Hey spouse, I'm not OK with raised voices during conflict. When voices are raised I will pause our discussion and take a 30-minute walk around the neighborhood alone. We can continue the discussion when I return."

Next, set your boundaries with your spouse. This is best done when your spouse's mood and mind are in a more calm state. It is also recommended that there be a level of agreement between you and your spouse. Are you willing to only be on a walk for fifteen minutes, instead of thirty?

Then, keep your boundaries. If you don't respect your own boundaries, your spouse won't respect them either. And their mental illness may exacerbate the situation.

Finally, give yourself grace. You will make mistakes as you learn to set boundaries in your marriage. Remember your boundary, reinforce it and apply it again.

You may also consider, and I highly recommend, that you work with a therapist to develop your boundaries.

7

Self-Care Is Not Cliché

4 Self-Care Methods I Use (+1 I Should Have)

Self-care is important for your mental health and well-being in any stressful circumstance.

When bipolar and dissociation enters your marriage, however, stress has a whole new meaning. Everything you thought you knew about life, your partner, and yourself is challenged. Your response to mania, depression, and alters becomes your identity. It becomes all consuming; trying to fix everything while walking on eggshells. Eventually, you forget who you are.

If you don't prioritize your self-care, then you will lose yourself.

That was me.

Everything I ever loved, that made me me, was gone.

Hobbies are gone. Interests vanished. Isolation triumphed.

I don't recognize myself anymore.

Although it took time, I did eventually reclaim myself.

Here are the 4 self-care methods I found most beneficial for me (and 1 I wish I had done more of):

Writing in a Journal. I began writing everything that was going on. Writing in a journal helped me process what was happening. And I got my thoughts and feelings out so they would no longer be stuck in my mind. One thing I would have done differently was journal about good times in the midst of the darkness. They were there, but I didn't record them.

Art. I found being creative a great outlet. I tried various arts and crafts. Acrylic paints. Sketching. Photography. Coloring. Each of these gave me a sense of control for a brief moment. And I cherished the calmness. Creating is a joy for me.

Walking. Prioritizing walking at the beginning of the day for at least 30 minutes (I often did 45 minutes, though) was critical. My days were always difficult if I didn't walk. This became a non-negotiable for me. Walking outside was always best, too.

Hot Bath. Sitting in a hot bath helped the stress melt away. If the water became cold, I would drain it and run more hot water. Nothing wrong with a two-hour hot bath, the way I see it.

These four self-care methods helped ground me. They also rejuvenated me and gave me strength for another day, even just another hour.

But I denied myself another method of self-care.

When my partner was manic, it was like a label was stamped on my forehead for the world to see. I feared what the world thought. So, I opted for loneliness and isolation.

What I needed was my friends.

Friends. There are people who love me for me. But I didn't love me, because I lost who I was. So, I lost all confidence to reach out. I tried, and there were a couple of times where I did. But I needed more time with friends.

In time I reclaimed myself. But I didn't reclaim what I lost. I reclaimed what I became. And I like who I am getting to know.

6 Ways to Focus On You and Improve Your Mental Health

Prioritize yourself. What are the "nonnegotiable" items for your physical, mental, emotional, and spiritual health? The more you take care of yourself, the more strength you have for others. This means learning how to set boundaries and saying no.

Expand on hobbies and interests you have. Try new things. Examples might be taking a dance class, or a painting class, or a writing workshop, or putting together a wooden ship model. Perhaps it's team sports. These experiences don't have to become a long-term part of your life, but they will mold your character.

Continue learning. If you're in school, strive to do well. But, in addition, learn more about topics not a part of your school curriculum. May I suggest that one topic you learn is personal finance. Learn how money works. Learn how to write and keep a budget, balance a checkbook (what's that?), avoid debt, have an emergency fund, save for short-term purchases, save for long-term purchases, and invest for your future. Learn that money comes from work. So,…

Work. If work is your identified source of mental stress, then work to make a change. Whatever your work is now, it doesn't have to be your career, it's just work. You'll learn how to interact with others, gain new skills, be responsible, and perhaps even lead. Work (with the right mindset) can be rejuvenating.

Maintain and develop friendships. Relationships do not inherently equal isolation. If you are married/dating, cherish your time together, but don't ostracize your friends. You don't have to become a socialite. If you are introverted, like I am, a few close friends is all you need.

Find ways to serve others. Keep this small to start out. For example, we keep small snacks and drinks in our car to give to the homeless. Smile and say hi to people you don't know. Wave to someone as they drive past you in your neighborhood. Open the door for someone else.

These are little Acts of Random Kindness that become ark's for those in the flood of so many trials our world is facing right now.

8

Success Reimagined

Yes, you can have a successful relationship even if it is marred by mental illness. But before I address what my marriage looks like today (approximately five years after the first hospitalization at the time of publishing), I want to acknowledge that not all relationships arrive where we are.

This journey is difficult and it is long. From 2018 - 2021 I considered ending the marriage four times. Many relationships do end. That is unfortunate, but may be the right thing. Only you can answer that.

For two and a half years my spouse did not have the proper medication regimen and treatment plan, because all of this is resolved through trial and error. It took another one to one and a half years for us to begin really working on our marriage again.

We also are very cognizant that we have no idea what the future holds. Life is unpredictable and mental illness compounds the unpredictability. Stability happened - this time. Life is stable - right now. But our bodies and life circumstances change over time. What is working now may not work in the future. But right now, we continue to work together.

Even though I considered leaving, one of the reasons I stayed was that my spouse never gave up and owned the journey to embrace the unknown. I really appreciate that my spouse grew into the following:

Actively sticks to the treatment plan.

- Keeping the prescribed medicine regimen,
- Prioritizing sleep, and
- Committing to individual and couples therapy.

Actively participates in the care of the home.

We do not have defined chores. We work together for a clean house. I modified my expectations and ideas of what it means to have a clean house. My spouse adjusted expectations on the responsibilities of having a clean house. It is a partnership.

Actively participates in the raising of our three children.

This one is easy for both of us, and is a strength in our relationship.

Actively contributes to the financial success of our family.

Both of us are employed full-time in careers that bring value to us.

Acknowledges the impact the symptoms of mental illness had on me.

My spouse also listened to the audio book When Someone You Love Is Bipolar. Afterwards my spouse came to me and said, "I don't know which to tell you - 'I am sorry' or 'Thank you.'" What a sweet realization; it meant so much to me to hear that.

I, too, have experienced a season of growth, have owned my journey, and am striving to embrace the unknown.

Because of the nature of being a caretaker, I did pretty much everything. As my spouse improved I was asked what I needed help with. I was so used to doing everything myself that I responded, sometimes in frustration, "I've got this. Thanks!" As I realized that my spouse was genuine in the request I adjusted to responding with, "Thanks for asking. Let me think about it." Today, my response to this query is with one or two items that need doing and am confident will get done.

I changed my mindset around expectations. I used to say that I had to lower my expectations. But this always made me feel like I was defeated, like I was also losing my standards and identity. I no longer say that I am lowering or raising my expectations; rather, I modify my expectations. The reality is that life is dynamic and our circumstances are fluid with mental illness. So expectations are modified to the season of life we are in.

I accepted that my spouse needs sleep. This translates into early bedtimes, sleeping in on the weekends, and more alone time for me. I used to classify this as laziness. My spouse isn't lazy, however. My spouse just needs sleep. Although we don't do as much together as we did before, the time we do spend together is full of love, kindness, and support.

I learned to communicate. Whereas my spouse over communicates, I hardly communicate. I first began to express my feelings through various forms of journal writing. I had so many emotions, thoughts, and feelings bottled up that I, too, was hurting within. Now, I am able to express myself and share with my spouse what I am experiencing and desiring. This has strengthened our marriage tremendously.

As you've read, my journey has been painful, and it came out of nowhere. Committing to support my spouse through the unknown of the future is a big part of what marriage is all about. We truly had to embrace the unknown. As a result, we have reimagined our marriage and have established a beautiful family. And that is my hope for you.

If you found this book relatable, and perhaps beneficial and hopeful, I would appreciate a kind and favorable review from you on Amazon.